# PANTHEISM

*And other Essays*

By
"L. E. C."

(Louisa Emily Cohen)

KENNIKAT PRESS
Port Washington, N. Y./London

PANTHEISM

First published in 1926
Reissued in 1971 by Kennikat Press
Library of Congress Catalog Card No: 79-118531
ISBN 0-8046-1154-8

Manufactured by Taylor Publishing Company    Dallas, Texas

# CONTENTS

## PREFACE

These essays of a pantheist may perhaps be a help to men who doubt and search because they are unable to reconcile their idea of an Almighty and Beneficent God with the existence of evil and pain. They are not written for those who are at peace with themselves and the world.

# PROLOGUE

Philosophy and Science, like two rivers, pursue their course towards the Sea of Truth. The waters of philosophy flow in quick descent, past rocks and rolling stones, and brook no hindrance. Science, slow and patient, gathers on her way all rivulets of knowledge, forms dark and silent pools wherein she rests to prove her turgid waves and what's opaque is left to sink. So passes on until she meets philosophy. Then each helps each to make a deeper bed, the wisdom of mankind.

# PANTHEISM

## I.—INTRODUCTION

MEN seem to feel more keenly now than in the past that all truths are akin, and they realise better the need to unify knowledge, notwithstanding, may be because of, the growing complexity of research. No doubt there was always the same desire to be consistent, but in a former age men had to face obstacles of which some have disappeared. Theology, Philosophy and Science were then in water-tight compartments. Theology was quick to perceive and resent any theory which conflicted with her doctrines, and would assert her infallibility with little fear of opposition.

But times have changed. The three branches

of knowledge still keep within their own domain, but whether because the world has become more enlightened, or because science and its methods have affected the general outlook, there is evidence of a wish to throw aside prejudice and to combine in the search after truth. Such openmindedness should above all favour philosophy, which may be expected to make valuable contributions to synthetic knowledge, especially in the region of psychology, as speculative minds have a natural aptitude for that science. But the principal work of the philosopher must ever be to gather truth from all sources, with which to build a theory of the cosmos.

Inevitably such theory will be but a faint reflex of the reality, a translation into the language of man. It cannot be an adequate explanation of the universe ; it will at most express some fleeting aspects of the phenomena of " mind " and " matter " and the conclusions it may draw therefrom. For the part cannot embrace the whole. The philosopher should put into his own language some of the discoveries of science and even the experiences of theology, and this he can do by means of fruitful analysis and generalisations ; it is for him to show that the philosopher, the theologian and the man of science perceive different aspects of the same truth.

In the following essay, the writer suggests a theory of the unity of the cosmos and he also suggests that religion is a continuous revelation, which includes the discoveries of science.

For the sake of conciseness, he has not stayed to qualify some of his assertions, and he pleads this in excuse of any apparent dogmatism. It should be added that, while he has striven for a consistency without which no theory can hope to be convincing, he is aware that consistency alone is but a form of logic, and that its outcome can be no greater than the mental stuff which has suggested the hypothesis on which his theory is based. The title of the following paper, " Esoteric Pantheism," is meant to express the point of view that God is the universe and that He and man must be thought of as inside not outside it. The writer believes that men's reasoning power and imagination will be used to better purpose when working from within outwards, than if they take an exoteric stand as imaginary spectators of the cosmos. This will be explained presently.

Certain hypotheses have been laid down of which some may be, if not new, yet dressed in modern garb. If there is a grain of truth in this conception of the universe, it may perhaps bear fruit of which the seeds will live for a short span in the eternal sequence of events.

## II.—ESOTERIC PANTHEISM

It is well to state at once the hypotheses on which the writer has based his philosophy. All theories of religion and philosophy must rest upon hypotheses, conscious or not, and in this case the stating of them at the outset will clear away the cobwebs, and will enable the reader to take his bearings and close the book if he is so minded.

### Hypotheses

1  God is the cosmos.
2  Creation is transformation.
3  Evil *is*, therefore must be.

4 There was no beginning ; there will be no end.

5 Mind and matter are one.

Pantheism does not depend upon hypothesis 5 for even if spirit and life should be of a different nature from matter and not transformable each into the other, yet they are part of God manifested as spirit, life and matter, which idea alone constitutes pantheism.

### *Pantheism by Analogy*

Although pantheism is an ancient creed, it is only in our day, and owing to the discoveries of science, that it can claim to be supported by analogy, a point to be explained and developed presently. The intuitive and reasoning powers, and that sense of logic which gave birth to pantheism in the past, must surely be equally active now, and would, even without the new analogy, prevent it from being submerged either by the beliefs of established religions, or by that modern scepticism which is due, in many instances, to the growth of science.

Pantheism might be expected to appeal to philosophers rather than to the masses, because its hypothesis that God and the universe are one is unfamiliar, possibly also unattractive. On the other hand the present time is, for various reasons, favourable to a belief in pantheism. For the old gods are discredited and there are none to take their place. So now more than ever " 'Tis time new hopes should animate the world." The theory of evolution has supplanted the ancient belief that man was made in God's image. In vain the churches teach that religion and science are not incompatible. The people doubt ; their faith is shaken, their ideals lowered. They want a God whom they can love and in whom they can believe. The saner spirits view with alarm the abyss towards which the world is drifting, self-determination and irreligion marching hand in hand—whither ?

Formerly, and because men have ever been susceptible to argument through analogy, they believed in the fatherhood of God, in His personality by analogy with themselves, and believed that they were created in His image. Now that they have been told of their ancient, yet lowly descent, their belief in God, which was founded on this analogy, has been weakened or destroyed. More than ever they are alive to the existence of evil and injustice ; and they have ceased to believe that the world has been created by a beneficent and almighty God. The foundations of their ancient creeds have been roughly shaken, and the people's myriad hands are pulling down the edifice amidst rude, though mirthless, laughter. For they suffer, being godless. Religion is more than a belief and a philosophy, it is, and has ever been, a guide, a safeguard and a consolation. If men could interpret their own half-formed thoughts and could gauge their utmost needs, they might well exclaim : " Our gods are destroyed, give us others in their stead. . . . "

### *The creed of the pantheist*

The neo-pantheist founds his belief on Intuition, Reason and Analogy. Postulating his oneness with God, intuition and inspiration are to him the outcome of this hypothesis, and the faculty which enables him to receive inspiration—

by the discoveries of science. Here we may
pause for a moment to wonder at the intuition
which in past ages prompted men to feel or guess
at their oneness with God before science had
shown them throughout life the analogy of that
oneness.

That analogy between God and man, and probably between him and every form of organized
life, is all but complete. For living beings are
complexes of lives, cells, animalcules, and each
being is at once the whole, and the sum of the
parts. Man is conscious, or subconscious, of
these organisms that are his personality, although
he thinks, feels and lives in terms of one. Though
in a sense conscious, he is not cognizant of his
complex ego, by which is meant that he does not
interpret or understand his consciousness, for it
is just this complex which is himself and which
gives him the sense of unity and completeness.
Of this fact, a feeble illustration is the vision of his
two eyes, the breath of his two nostrils felt and
thought of as one image, one breathing.

Yet the analogy between God and man is not
absolutely complete. Because God is the whole

of which man is the fraction, even so, man is conscious of his non ego,[1] whereas God, as the total consciousness, has no non ego. It may be that each one of us, with our small joys and sorrows, is felt by God to be part of Himself, and such indeed is the writer's belief.

The common idea of God as a Person apart from the universe and separate from it, is founded by analogy on men's experience of separate individuals of whom each is a non ego to all others— this idea they have transferred to God. It will be dealt with further under " Time " and " Space." In contrast to this belief is that of the pantheist, who realises both his incompleteness and his oneness or unity. It may even be that in some distant, latent way, man is conscious or might become conscious of the whole of his non ego.[2] With regard to the analogy between God and

[1] The truth of men's impression of a world outside of them has been questioned, and may be an unproved conclusion, but the writer is not concerned with it, as according to his creed, which also, it is admitted, cannot be proved, men, as part of the cosmos, are in touch with other parts. Therefore, to the pantheist, men's consciousness of their non ego requires no proof, being founded on hypothesis 1.

[2] See Some of our Faculties and Appendix, pages 94 and 101,

man, it is probable that every live cell in man has a measure of consciousness of which the total sums up the consciousness of man, which again is the nucleus of his complex.[1]

Under section " Free Will," man is described as the arbiter of his fate ; and herein, by analogy, he is like God, who is the arbiter of the whole. It may be that when men better understand their own psychology, which, after all, is the real origin of their beliefs, they will be drawn towards the simple creed of the pantheist.

### III.——PHILOSOPHY OF PANTHEISM

Most religions and philosophies have sought to explain something more than passing phenomena, to get further back in the sequence of events, back to a beginning and a cause. But as a beginning of anything is inconceivable, some have supposed a creation and a Creator, of whom they have predicated that He had no beginning.      These postulates are unsatisfying,

[1]It is unnecessary to labour the point that man is not cognizant of all parts of himself, and more especially during sleep ; this, however, is a question for the physiologist.

because they do not touch the problem of a material world created out of nothing. Nor does the conception of God as a perfect, infinite, almighty Spirit, the Creator of the world, account for the existence of evil ; and so men have imagined a spirit of evil. Indeed the historic religions would seem to be incomplete without a personification of evil, though, as a fact, Satan does not loom so largely in our times as he did of yore. Still, the existence of evil troubles many persons as being incompatible with the perfection of God. Quite other is the pantheist's outlook. God and the cosmos being one, there was no beginning of either spirit or matter, therefore no creation. As for the existence of evil, since evil there is, it must be necessary. This idea is simple and pious. The pantheist accepts, not explains, a state of mind somewhat like resignation. But the acceptance of evil does not rule out the hope that the forces of good may increase as those of evil diminish. (See " Good and Evil " and " Mathematics in Man and Nature.")[1] He postulates little of God except by analogy through a process

[1] pages 42 and 51.

of inductive reasoning and in all humility. He knows that the mystery of the universe can never be unveiled, nor even fractions of it understood. These are assuredly as complex as the whole ; but even if they are not so, still our planet will probably have lived its life and our sun have grown cold, before the toil and patience of science will have unravelled the smallest portion of nature's tangled web. Humbly accepting his ignorance, the pantheist pauses to wonder how God can be thought of as anything but the whole, or how the whole can be anything but the sum of all the parts. In this belief he concludes that man and nature must be of the same substance as God, and in that postulate he seeks and finds his religion and philosophy.

If God is the cosmos, there was no creation and no beginning. But there is evolution, in which sense " creation " is continuous. All growth, all manifestations of life and consciousness, must be manifestations of God. All instances of the One and the Many are God manifested as the One and the Many ; manifested also as matter and spirit, whether these are combined in the stuff of the world as energy, or whether they are entities of different nature. In the latter case, it might follow that spirit is potent to permeate matter at a stage when matter is ready to receive it, or rather (as the writer is disposed to believe) that spirit is latent in matter at *all* stages and that the ultimate unit is spirit and matter combined.

A belief in the identity of matter, life and mind will doubtless bring upon the writer the accusations of materialism. The truth of this accusation cannot be admitted by one who holds that the stuff of substance or energy, its ultimate essence, is as much beyond man's ken as is " spirit," supposing that the two are not identical. In any case, the idea of their identity, or of their transformation, has in it nothing in common with materialism as generally understood. But the writer's view differs from that of the pure transcendentalist in that the former believes in the existence of the missing or scarce discovered links in evolution between matter and life, together with all that life includes. These links in evolution may yet be found. When they are found it will not seem far-fetched to assert that in *all* matter

or energy there is latent life and spirit, and it will
be re-asserted that " nature makes no leaps."
The prevailing idea of life is associated with birth
and death ; to the pantheist these events are
illustrations of his belief.    For the life of the seed
is part of the parent life.    An " individual "
plant may be propagated by cuttings or self-
rooting without cessation, without beginning or
end of any particular life, which is thus merged in
a continuous life.    Indeed there is no such thing
as a separate individual life either in time or space.
If the problem of the inheritance of acquired
characteristics has not been finally settled, and if
the answer should eventually be in favour of such
inheritance, it would follow that psychic life is
one with previous psychic lives (as it certainly is
in regard to ideas), the good and evil actions in
such lives affecting, through inherited tendencies,
subsequent generations.[1]    At the risk of a weari-
some repetition, it may be said that such continuous stream of life, which unites in itself successive
units of life, is to the pantheist part of the life of

[1]This possibility raises the question of personal responsibility.    (See ' 'Free Will," page 32.)

God, which is the one complete everlasting individual life.

It is possible that this question of continuity and discontinuity in life may in some way be connected with the Quantum theory which, if we have understood its drift, states that energy is discontinuous and proceeds by jerks.  The analogy would be in the separateness of individual lives, yet in the continuity of the stream of life through parenthood or otherwise.

### IV.—THE ONE AND THE MANY

We are faced everywhere with the one and the many, with the organism and its component parts.  They confront us in the skies as myriads of stars, held in equilibrium by some universal force or energy or necessity, which combines these myriads into one whole, the universe ; in· man and animals, where the individual is a complex of live cells, in man again, as the individual and the race, in man's· mental complex, where his many wills, desires and thoughts revolve round some spiritual principle of unity.[1]

[1]See " Free Will," page 32.

We see the one and the many in human institutions, in nations of which each citizen is a unit, in towns, villages, schools, families, religions, political parties and so forth. All such instances are analogous to live organisms. For they are held together, cemented by ideas or affection, by laws or loyalty, and through them all runs the same principle of separate units forming one whole. The One composed of the Many, each unit of which is part of the One. Even in such infinitesimally small particles as the atom, which was guessed at by the ancients and has been discovered by modern science, the same principle holds good ; the one and the many, separate yet combined. This fact, which permeates all nature from constellations of stars to constituents of atoms, is the universal *analogy* in which pantheism finds its logic.

### V.——SUBJECTIVE AND OBJECTIVE IDEAS AND THE NATURE OF PRAYER

It is common to treat subjective and objective ideas as if they were divided by a hard and fast line. This point of view, applied to prayer, is often the cause of scepticism in those who regard religious experiences as " subjective." According to the pantheist, inasmuch as God and the cosmos are one, " subjective " and " objective " facts are interdependent. Every feeling, sense or emotion is at once subjective and objective ; the former because it is felt as part of consciousness, the latter because there is reaction to something " inside " or outside the individual. The word " inside " is here taken as meaning some part of the individual himself other than his consciousness of the emotion in question. It is not intended to convey that there is no difference in the nature or cause of objective ideas or that " objective " and " subjective " ideas are altogether indistinguishable. A man may rise with a bitter taste in his mouth and rightly conjecture that he is suffering from indigestion (subjective), and not that he has suddenly tasted bitter aloes (objective) ; or he may feel depressed on account of family and other worries (objective), or depressed from some unknown cause, in which case he may rightly lay the blame on his liver (subjective). Such cases might be considered respectively to be due to objective and subjective states of mind, distinctions which are convenient in everyday life, but need to be qualified before the pantheist can accept them. Given that a man is a complex with a principle of unity, a centre of control,[1] the bitter taste in his mouth, which results from indigestion, is both objective and subjective ; objective because produced by a defective organ which, although part of him, is not himself ; subjective because he is conscious of it, though he may be unaware of the cause. But it is objective in a different way from the bitter aloes, for these, unlike his defective organ, are not part of him.

The depression due to family worries is objective, whereas the depression which has no obvious cause is subjective by definition, but it is also objective, even if it is due to an untraced source ; this source may be thunder in the air, or diet, or excitement, or stimulants, or idleness, or any of a thousand possible reasons within or without the man. If the cause is within him, still it is objective, though not quite in the same sense as if the cause is outside of him. In other words,

[1] See " Free Will," page 32.

subjective experiences must have objective causes within or without, a point of the utmost importance when prayer is considered. In virtue of his creed, the pantheist believes in the possibility of communion with God, and contends that religious men of all creeds may experience emotions which convince them, and rightly, that they are in touch —so to say—with God. To such assertions it has been objected that these religious emotions are subjective. It is clear that neither the evidence adduced, nor the objections to it, can be proved, but the pantheist's position being derived logically from his postulates is at any rate consistent. If during prayer he feels nearer to God and more conscious of God, he has no reason to doubt that his emotion is objective in the usual sense as well as subjective, and that somehow he is closer to the great Centre. Further, if his creed should be a nearer approach to the truth than other creeds, that fact would or might give greater force to his experiences, for a thought, like a feeling, is a force. Moreover, his argument against the mere subjectivity of prayer is more consistent, if not than that of men who are deter-

minists and deny spirit altogether, yet more so
than the argument of those who, while believing
in both spirit and matter, yet maintain that religious experiences are subjective, otherwise a
delusion. That there are delusions, as in mad-
ness, delirium, hysteria and so on, is not disputed,
but these scarcely affect the point. So the pantheist believes in the objectivity of religious experiences, and that he is, through them, brought
into closer touch with God. Yet no sane man in
the exercise of his unbiased judgment can feel
absolutely convinced that his judgment is transcendental, that his premises are sound and his
conclusions undeniable : when he has felt and
thought and felt again, what after all is his logic ?
He knows that the Truth is beyond him as it is
beyond all men, but in his doubt he will turn again
to prayer as the source of such wisdom as he is
capable of receiving.

VI.—A PANTHEIST'S PRAYER TO THE UNKNOWABLE
GOD

Let me wonder and pray, even I who am a
fraction of Thy Godhead, who am as nought,

so small is my knowledge and my strength. Yet
it is fit that I should love and pray, for in Thy light
I shall grow ; nor shall I be blinded, for what
Thou grantest to me is measured to my size and is
not more than I can grasp. I will pray and rest
and sleep, one with my God.

## VII.——SPACE AND TIME

To understand one's tools is a first step in
philosophy as in other arts ; moreover, the
philosopher's tools are complex, consisting as they
do, of the mentality or psychology of men. He
has to discover what in common thought is mere
adaptation to surroundings or abstraction from
the objective world. To do this effectually, he
must first discard the well-worn garments of inherited thought and language. He must do this
in order to understand the psychology of men,
his own included. Possibly then he may distinguish what are unconscious abstractions, and
what truth underlies men's unprobed convictions.
Especially is careful analysis imperative when
considering such ideas as space and time. For
these are, properly speaking, attributes or pro-

ducts of mind.  Space and time have occupied
men's thoughts from the earliest days, and of late
the study of these subjects has received a new
impetus from the theories associated particularly
with the name of Professor Einstein.  But even
the man in the street, let alone the philosopher,
has decided ideas about Space and Time, and it
is proposed to consider here his point of view.

We should say, then, that the idea of empty
space is an abstraction.  What one sees are
objects which appear to be divided by distance in
various directions.  This distance is conceived
as empty space before the idea of the surrounding
air has been gained.  The first impression is that
of objects carved out of a frame of emptiness of
three dimensions, whether in a room, in the open
or in the sky.  But this idea of empty space is
different from most abstractions.  The first, or
parent idea, is that of the extension of objects.
The second idea (that of space) is the negative of
the idea of extension, or, more exactly, a minus
quantity.  For the shape carved by objects in
emptiness is the same as that of the objects themselves, even as a design cut from a sheet of paper

leaves its two dimensional form negatively (or in minus quantity) in the framework of paper. In the same way the surrounding walls of a bare room shape the emptiness or space within them. Bring in a table and you alter the shape of the space in the room, because the table is now carved out of it. So it is that the notion of the space in the room may be described psychologically as the unconscious negative of that of objects in the room which it outlines. When the notion of emptiness is replaced by that of air, it is not altered in any marked way, for what we have called the negative idea of space, which has now become the positive idea of air, will presently be transferred from air to empty space in general, outside our planet's air, and finally to " infinite " space. It follows that as emptiness has not been recognized as a negative, it has been thought of as an entity. This is not wonderful, for one is constantly reminded of the form of space by the objects which surround it, or which make dents into it, and as this experience dates from early childhood through the senses of touch and sight, it has all the force of early impressions.

Touching the absence of limits to space, called infinity, this idea is also derived from the shape of objects. Everything one sees has limits. The stars are carved out of space and limited. If one travels in imagination to the confines of the universe, one probably thinks that, however numerous the stars, there yet must be a sort of general outline of the starry universe, and then it is one imagines illimitable empty space beyond. Or one may try to imagine an infinite universe of stars floating in infinite space. Or if a man believes in the ether, this will make no difference, for he will think of ether as floating in infinite space, or as being itself infinite, in which case it becomes (in thought) another name for space. Thus his imagination is brought to a standstill by the idea of the infinite extension of ether or the infinite extension of space. It is true that the word infinite conveys little but a negative, yet man finds it simpler to think of an infinite universe in infinite space than of a finite universe and finite space. Some men are satisfied with the thought of a finite number of stars, provided infinite space is granted. For the pantheist this difficulty does not arise because he has trained himself to take an inside, an esoteric, view of the cosmos. He does not think of it as a whole, while conceiving himself as an imaginary spectator outside of it, because to him, the cosmos is God, of which he himself is a fraction, and his imagination is trained to think from *inside outwards*, to the distant stars, if he will, or towards the utmost limits of the ether. It is easier thus to grasp the notion that there is *no* outside, that the limits are inside, that infinite space is a fiction of the brain, born of the experience of getting outside of objects, of seeing them limited by other objects or by space. When this fiction is recognized as such, the esoteric view can be taken. Again, if God is the whole, how can there be anything outside of God ; how can there be that " space," which is confessedly emptiness, otherwise nothing ? Men have made an entity of space, it is an obsession difficult to eject.[1]  An objection has been raised that it is

[1]Professor Einstein's theory of the curvature of space has been accepted by mathematicians and physicists. It does not seem to be in any way inconsistent with the conception of the universe suggested by the writer, provided that the idea of ether is substituted for that of space.

impossible to imagine a point at the limits of the universe where an arm could not be thrust outside that limit into the void. The pantheist thinks this a mistaken view, for there *is* no outside. The mind must be trained to feel itself inside. The idea of the infinity of space is " subjective," in the ordinary sense of the word, and is based on nothing more than the difficulty of picturing its opposite, namely, the finality of extension. The way out of this dilemma is to take what is here called the esoteric view, and this is possibly a mere matter of training and habit.

The idea of time, like that of space, is to be regarded as the outcome of men's psychology. The reality, of which time is the symbol, can be expressed in many ways ; as events in sequence, as transformation, repetition, energy in action or simply energy. But static energy is not, as a rule, manifest to men. Time is in truth the measuring rod of events, a symbol, and as such useful. But it is not the entity which many believe it to be. They see changing events, beginnings and endings, while the sun turns in the heavens and the hands of clocks move round.

Hunger and sleep recur at intervals, for all in nature is rhythmic, and to these intervals men have given the appropriate name of time. And they carry watches ! If a man feels bored, he says that time hangs, while his dog stretches himself, or sleeps, or, with pleading eyes, begs to be taken for a run ; the dog thinks in terms of yawns and of longing for change and exercise ; his master in terms of time. To realise that time is an abstraction, not an entity, it suffices to imagine that there is no universe, therefore neither events nor energy, in fact, nothing. Surely, then, time also would be non-existent. Yet there are some who look upon time as a reality, a thing pursuing its course independently of all else. Have they not left psychology out of count and men's brains which have created time ?

It has been objected that the words " sequence of events " *are* time, but a sequence of events is truly either a repetition, or a transformation or metamorphosis, as shown by the life history of the moth, which, in common parlance, takes time. It is probable that even in extinct stars, matter is synonymous with energy ; but if not, and if there be such a thing as quiescent matter, then in those dead stars there would be no time because no energy, no action, no events.

The writer's definition of " time " in psychology (its only mode of existence) is an unconscious replica in negative of the sequence of events, in fact, a frame of measurement, events making dents into it figuratively, as it has been suggested of objects that they make dents in space.

For practical purposes the " duration " or successive number of events needs to be measured, by a common denominator, as the value of objects is measured in terms of money. This comparison might pass without comment, but that money has intrinsic value as metal or credit, whereas " time " has no objective reality and is valuable only indirectly for its convenience to men in directing their lives. Indeed, without measurement by " time," our complex civilization would be impossible. The hour-glass and sundial are illustrations of events symbolizing time, or, as one says, " taking time." If there exist in nature units of energy, such units can easily be conceived as exact repetitions, and their " jerks " as being

regular.[1]   They could be regarded as events in-
volving time ;   thus measurements might be
either in terms of energy or of time or of number.
But yet energy, not time, would be the entity.
Probably all activity inherent in matter is measurable symbolically by time.   The sequence of
events in the universe should be thought of as a
revolving circle or continuous action without beginning or end.

As for the duration of the cosmos, it would
follow that substance and energy, as sequence of
events, are, always have been, always will be, to
use the common parlance of past, present and
future.   Given matter, its changes or forces, the
idea of time is superfluous.   For the changes of
matter fill up or are time, as matter fills up or is
the universe.[2]

[1]See Quantum Theory, page 58.

[2]Should the cosmos be conceived as taking up less space
by shrinkage, still there would be no space outside of the cosmos,
for " space " would shrink with the substance, or supposing
ether instead of space to fill up all interstices of substance, the
contingency of shrinkage would not seem to arise ; but if it did,
and if the universe and the ether were to shrink, there would be
no space outside them.   These theories may be left to the
reader's judgment, for comparison with the more usual ones of

These unceasing forces of the cosmos suggest a speculation ; are the forces of energy inter-destructive, and is the universe, as the theatre of this civil war, becoming comatose ? In that case, will the remote consequences be chaos (or equilibrium) until a new cycle of activity, a new cosmos arises ? Even then nothing would be changed—for God and the universe would still be one.

### VIII.—FREE WILL

The question of personal responsibility will be argued in this short section from a pantheist's point of view, but in stating his theories, the writer must qualify them in regard to hypothesis 5 by pointing out again that the essence of pantheism does not depend upon that hypothesis.

Although, or perhaps because, he is a trans-cendentalist, he believes in the kinship, not to say in the identity of spirit and matter. He holds that matter will ever transcend complete know-

a creation (which pre-supposes time as antecedent to it), and a universe floating in infinite space. Such space would then be supposed to have " existed " before the universe occupied a part of it ledge and analysis, if only because he believes that within its complex there is either present or latent life. (This belief is based upon the hypothesis that God and nature are one.) If *life*, then also *will*, would be included in the very stuff of matter and from will to freedom is but a step. Some say that freedom is a fiction of the brain which has been evolved for its usefulness. Although not denying its usefulness, the writer does not believe that it is a fiction, for he attaches weight to men's *feeling* of freedom, which he regards as part of their consciousness, while admitting that on his own showing this " subjective " feeling or intuition may have its " objective " side within, in the shape of various desires or motives. Still, and comparing values, he notes how deeply men are moved by that sense of responsibility which to them is the only possible attitude towards life. Therefore, believing though he does that every thought, motive or will are forces, be they ever so contradictory, he postulates that there is in man a central will, the free arbiter round which those forces revolve. (The last word is used more or less figuratively.)

The hypothesis of a central will accords with his main belief, the one and the many, inseparable yet distinct. Mention has been made of the possibility of spirit merging itself into matter when, through evolution, matter should be in a state to receive it.[1] But this theory seems far-fetched and appeals to the writer less than that of spirit always latent in matter ; also it would imply separate units of spirit and matter. To sum up ; mind and matter are one and transcendental ; matter develops into conscious mind through the evolution of life ; will and freedom become synonymous at some stage of evolution, and freedom, like life, contains a central principle.

Comparing the position of the pantheist with that of the materialist, both believe in the evolution of matter into life, but whereas the materialist or determinist sees in motives the action of blind forces, the stronger prevailing, thus ruling out free will—the pantheist awaits the discovery of the missing link between matter and life in order to establish beyond question the transcendental nature of matter. Any failure to find the missing

[1]Philosophy of Pantheism, page 12.

link would however leave him unmoved, convinced as he is that his theories will in due course be supported by science or, in other words, that science will tend to corroborate those facts which are taken for granted by his postulates. These postulates are the identity of God and the universe and the transcendental nature of both mind and matter. In the event of a complete equation of matter being found, it would no doubt be asserted that such discovery must banish the idea of latent life, or anyhow of transcendentalism in matter and therefore of free will. The rejoinder to that assertion would be that the completeness of the equation could never be proved, because, in the final analysis of matter or energy, some latent life might have escaped our weighing and measuring machines, and there might yet be in matter something more than had been discovered by science. So in either contingency, that of a failure to find the missing link, or that of a successful discovery of a complete equation of matter, the writer may claim that free will cannot be disproved and that a belief in freedom is consistent with the postulates of his creed.

IX.—PSYCHOLOGY, PHILOSOPHY AND RELIGION

These subjects are interdependent. As a philosopher deals primarily with causes or sequences of events, he should be a psychologist for the reason that the psychology of a man comes earlier in the " sequence " than the product of his brain—his philosophy ; he must, therefore, understand himself, if he is to understand what he produces. As to religion and philosophy, they are inseparable, because in every religion a philosophy is implicit. Moreover, philosophy itself, is woven into the language commonly used, that is learned in childhood and, together with the ideas which it connotes, becomes part of a man's mental equipment, and has a large share in determining his beliefs.[1] Unless, therefore, he is naturally analytic and sceptical about ready-made ideas, language will influence his philosophic and religious views, hence also his psychology. Other factors are his nature as inherited, and his education : in his nature must be included his various faculties, of which the highest is the re-

[1]See Language, page 77

ligious one, and it should be repeated that all religious men are psychologically related, whatever
may be their creeds.  As to the pantheist, he
should be open-minded beyond men of other
religions, who, for the most part, hold a creed
they have been taught in childhood.  From this it
would follow that their beliefs and even their
religious feelings must be coloured and predeter-
mined in a given direction.  But the pantheist
who has broken away from the old religions has
probably cleared his brain of prejudices and at
this stage he must find his bearings in the maze
of life's problems ;  he will need to tread his in-
tricate path with hesitating steps ;  but he will be
open-minded and indulgent because his creed
teaches him to regard all men as brothers.  If he
has conquered his freedom of thought by intuition
and religious inspiration, although he is in a
(religious) minority, he need have little fear that
he will go far wrong.  But if he has adopted
pantheism because it appeals to his reason, and
if he does not belong to the inspired brotherhood,
he must follow in the wake of those whose creed
he has adopted.  Happily men may differ in their

beliefs, yet agree on what constitutes a good or bad life, a consoling thought for anyone who may be in doubt whither his creed is leading him[1] ; and if he be diffident, he may recall the words of Marcus Aurelius : " Walk with a crutch if you will, but walk straight."

## X.—DEATH SURVIVAL

This subject is full of perplexity. To most of us it is one of extreme importance. If we felt sure of a continued existence as individuals after death, we should look with indifference on many events in our lives to which we now give exaggerated importance. Beyond all else, what troubles us is the thought that we may never meet again those we have loved. This doubt should not worry men whose religion instils into them a belief in a future life, yet it is strange how little satisfaction some people derive in this respect from their faith. But apart from these, there are many, both pantheists and others, who yearn for some assurance of a future life, some argument in favour of survival.

[1]See Good and Evil, page 42.

Unfortunately there is little evidence, if any, of survival—and what there is, is scarcely convincing. Such evidence as would be accepted in a court of law must not be expected ; all that one can ask for are the psychological experiences of trustworthy persons. The evidence of spiritualists is inconclusive and unconvincing, because telepathy might account for the phenomena which they adduce to prove that there is communication between the living and the dead. A medium is generally called in who may be only a link in a long chain of telepathy—quite unconscious, of course—the result of which would be that the whole life of the dead person, or any part of it, might be revealed at a " séance " even without the presence of a medium. This is easily conceived by imagining telepathy to take the form of spoken language instead of thought, between all living persons whom the dead had known. Imagine this language transmitted by wireless, and you can see how the mourners would be made acquainted with facts about their dead friend. Or, again, facts known to only one surviving friend might be transmitted telepathically from him to a medium or to other persons. So that the conclusions of spiritualists must be rejected, but of course without any reflection on their sincerity.

On this subject of survival, science is mute and intuition says little. As a psychological experience the following may be quoted :—it is that of a friend for whose good faith the writer can vouch. Having lost a near and dear relative, and while fervently praying for some token of survival, he saw clearly (in his mind's eye ?) the loved face with the well-known consoling smile. Alas, this experience may have been subjective in the sense in which this word is mostly used. And that little bit of evidence is all that the writer can produce. So he must look elsewhere in the hope of finding arguments consistent with his creed.

A survival in this world without memory, otherwise metempsychosis, seems unlikely and meaningless ; also, it would be no consolation. The writer is disposed to reject the hypothesis. A survival in this world with memory and consciousness is contrary to all evidence, and the idea cannot be entertained. If man survives in another world, where and what is that world ? Neo-pantheists,

who do not postulate a spiritual world apart from
material worlds, might suppose life to be continued
on some other planet.    If man survived in another
world he might be conceived as meeting there
friends who had been his contemporaries on this
earth ; for there would be no inconsistency in the
thought that the central governing part of a man,
that which is felt by him as his personality, together
with memory and consciousness, should survive
on some other planet, or, as has been suggested,
in the ether, or in a substitute for the ether.[1]
But there is another hypothesis, namely, that
man, after death, without losing his identity, is
drawn closer to God, who is at once the centre
and the whole of the cosmos.   The pantheist
claims that this idea of translation is not more far-
fetched, nay, is less so, than the widely-held belief
in material and spiritual worlds as separate entities,
different in their nature, although associated as

[1]We are aware that it might be objected that memory and
consciousness are part of the brain and that, after death, these
could not survive—to this our answer is that man has not solved,
never can or will solve, the whole problem of force or energy.
Consciousness and memory are forces, or energy.   Even if the
brain is dead, who shall say that the energy it gave forth is
extinct ?   Still we admit the force of the objection.

spirit and matter in this life. Believing that man is one with God here and now, he also believes that man will be one with God hereafter ; that the forces which were himself, possibly held to-together by their long kinship, will move nearer to God, he knows not where nor how. " He who created me once can surely recreate me," so wrote Erasmus Darwin. The pantheist does not believe in creation in that sense, but he believes in the evolution or metamorphosis of the individual, and that man will survive as part of God.

## XI.—GOOD AND EVIL

It is not proposed to give more than a mere outline of a subject, which, for adequate treatment, would need a volume. Good and Evil will be considered mainly in their psychological and philosophical aspects, because their ethical side is treated separately.[1] It is unnecessary, therefore, to distinguish virtue and vice in this paper from other forms of good and evil, such as pleasure and pain, joy and sorrow, and all else that men connect with the subject. The writer believes in the necessity of evil *here* and *now ;* he believes

[1]See " Ethics," page 68.

that the forces of good increase as those of evil decrease, and that this transformation is proceeding on the lines of progress. He does not use the words " forces of good and evil " only in a spiritual sense, but also in the more intimate, or, as some might say, " material " sense that comes of the writer's theory of the " stuff " of the cosmos. That " stuff " he regards as an assemblage of units of commingled mind and matter, in other words, as matter in which mind is either present or latent. His hope of improvement is based on the theory of evolution or of some other factor working towards the same end. But progress is difficult to prove and belief in it is largely temperamental. Great and good men, regarded as forces, make for increase of good, and it is argued that their power outweighs that of bad men for evil. This hypothesis is of wide application, otherwise, surely, there would be anarchy and chaos. The suggested balancing or measuring of good against evil is one with the writer's belief in an ultimate unit, which he regards as transcendental, and without which measurement would seem to be impossible. But the truth of this hypothesis cannot be proved. In all ages the problem of good and evil has occupied philosophers and theologians ; it occupies them still. As a solution, the ways of Providence have been declared inscrutable ; or ingenious explanations have been suggested, founded upon interpretations of dogmas. To not a few moderns, good and evil are steps in evolution, a view which may well be correct, but is not all-embracing, as indeed nothing can be. Many deny that there is progress, and among the latter may be counted some who belong to established religions, some who are by nature pessimists, as well as not a few open-minded persons who honestly fail to see any evidence of improvement. Proof either way must not be expected. Man sees such a minute fraction of the whole that he has nothing whereby to compare and gauge progress. Even if it were possible to establish that evolution tends in that direction, that science is doing more good for man and beast in times of peace than injury during war ; even if it could be shown that, with the passing of the centuries—our tiny measuring rods —good increases at the expense of evil, yet nothing can be known with certainty even of the future of our own planet, much less of other worlds, our brothers in the universe. We cannot know whether there are, on the earth or elsewhere, gigantic cycles of alternate periods of progress and relapse. Of the real ultimate meaning of good and evil, all that can be stated are ephemeral phenomena, or if something beyond these may be surmised, it is because, minute as we are, we still are fractions of God, from Whom come our intuitions and knowledge, together with our limitations.

So man must turn his vision to his more immediate surroundings in " time " and " space," hoping that his horizon will grow, and that some progress is on the way. We propose to show : (1) that good and evil are respectively transformable, and (2) that evil and pain are useful, even necessary.

Self-control, effort and kindred states of mind are often transformed into satisfaction, as when a man who is moved by passion in a righteous cause, does not relax his efforts until he has gained his end. In this he finds his reward ; for the pain of effort is transformed into the pleasure of rest or the satisfaction of self-approval. His strenuous and painful efforts are replaced by the joy of success, even if it be only the success of self-conquest. Should he meet with failure, he will at least have the compensation of feeling increased power. In man, and throughout nature, love conquers pain and transforms it. A man fighting for country and home transcends fear. A mother tending a sick child ignores or defies fatigue. A timid bird or beast will defend its young with a courage born of love. Most of us have seen some little creature terrified at the sight of danger, and have seen its fear turn first to anger, next to a triumphant defence of its young. And not less true is the converse. Evil natures find pleasure in cruelty ; their bad instincts when successful are transformed into pleasurable sensations. Successful greed and ambition are cases in point. Every satisfaction of a bad motive is evil turned into good. These words are, of course, used in the philosophical sense indicated, not in their ethical sense, for we are far away from ethics. It is unnecessary to multiply examples of the respective transforming of good and evil, or to give instances where the " good " of one is the " evil " of another. But it may be noted that the best people suffer in a world where things are adapted to the average, and where inferior beings are a burden on those whose support is a benefit to such weaklings. It may be asserted, as showing how inextricably tangled are good and evil, that egoism is as necessary as altruism, which is a case of the usefulness of evil, not exactly of its transformation. A total absence of egoism is often the hallmark of a weak character. It has been said : " A fool and his money are soon parted." And further, as to the necessity of pain, it has been remarked with truth that man could not exist without pain, which is his mentor from birth unto death : " The scalded child fears the fire."

What conclusions, if any, can be drawn from these facts and arguments ? Perhaps none with absolute certainty, except by those for whom a future existence in a spiritual world is a postulate of their creed, carrying with it rewards for their trials here below. Apart from such persons, the question of progress resolves itself into a hope, for some, into a conviction. Meanwhile, we have

wars, with their mingling of good and evil in
every conceivable form, evil predominating ; we
see vice and sin and disease, deserved and un-
deserved, and to the eternal question of those
for whom God is more than a name : " Why
is there evil ? " comes the answer : " Evil there
is, so evil there must be, and evil is necessary here
and now."

# OTHER ESSAYS

# MATHEMATICS IN NATURE AND MAN

IT is admitted that there is a mathematical basis in nature, although, according to modern science, nature does not in all respects conform to the exactness of Euclidian mathematics. If nature falls short of exactness only through contingencies, the problem will always be to discover what those contingencies are. This problem covers a wide field, extending, let us say, from so-called " space " and " time " to physics, to political economy, indeed, very probably to most of the intellectual subjects in which men are interested and in which they often find themselves confronted by the opposites :—exactness on the one hand, and what appears to be the reality of phenomena or contingencies on the other. Again, if nature is even approximately exact, there should be an ultimate unit of energy or some other unit. For it is difficult to conceive mathematics apart from measurement, and the latter apart from a unit by which to measure. We are not considering practical difficulties ; these may be beyond man's power to solve, but it is here contended that if there is in nature a mathematical basis, a unit of measurement is thereby implied, and to the philosopher this idea is of paramount importance. If a unit is granted as a hypothesis, a mechanistic view of the cosmos might seem to follow. Especially would the pantheist, who does not necessarily differentiate between mind and matter, have to defend his position and his claim to being a transcendentalist. He would contend that there may be in nature undiscovered units different from, though comparable to, positive and negative electricity. In that case, not only would measurement be conceivable, but such undiscovered factors might be a link between the animate and the inanimate world ; they might explain the apparent difference between mind and matter as well as other differences such as those of sex (unless, indeed, these have already been explained). It seems futile to suggest the unknown as an explanation of the known and to leave the problem at that, but men are always in the end brought to this dead stop, and the hypothesis of an unknown but measurable unit is less of a " leap " in nature than the widespread belief in spirit and matter as separate entities ; a belief founded, moreover, on an interpretation of revelation which is not all-convincing.

Under the heading of " Free Will and Responsibility " is suggested a transcendental, together with a mechanistic, view of the cosmos, because freedom need not mean an increase or decrease of the total, and under " Good and Evil " is suggested that these may balance each other, the total remaining unchanged.

With regard to mathematics in man, if they are implicit in substance, it will seem simple enough to the pantheist that some rare men should be gifted with the intuition of that science, even as other men are able to distinguish without effort the intervals of the musical scale. (See Music and Sense of Beauty.) But no doubt in the great majority of cases intuition is absent and men's reasoning power suffices for the comprehension of mathematics.

The question of exactness in nature and man is

one of measurement or numbers. In general, men use the symbol of numbers as a help to thought and memory, for, although the mathematics of nature may not be independent of numbers or their equivalent, it seems that numbers are often used by men as mere abstractions, which are tacked on to the realities from which they have been abstracted and are then thought of as entities, instead of as symbols. This applies equally to cardinal and ordinal numbers. In the mathematics of nature, numbers are no doubt entities, the result being different (for instance) according to the numbers of units in an atom. In the pure mathematics of men, they are also entities in a different sense; by which is meant that man's brain, being, according to the pantheist, probably of the same " stuff " as matter, animate and inanimate, it follows that the thoughts and abstractions of his brain are entities as much as any other form of energy is an entity. So abstract thoughts may, in that sense, be entities. But when numbers are applied to everyday things they suggest an exactness to which they are not entitled, and in such case we should distinguish them as abstract ideas which are not entities. As an example, the expression, " three chairs," seems to be an exact definition ; but in reality " three " is an abstraction, because the chairs are not exactly alike ; in other words, a number, as commonly used, is a symbol to aid thought by language, except when it is used in mathematics as a unit of measurement or energy, either in nature or in man's brain.

Ordinal numbers are derived from cardinal numbers and have no more real existence. The 5th wrangler certainly expresses a very real idea and has very real results in a man's life. But it is merely a convenient and incomplete way of stating what it would be otherwise impossible to express, namely, that a certain man has, by the decision of his examiners, succeeded better than the 6th, 7th or 8th wranglers, and less well than the 1st, 2nd, 3rd and 4th. But his position as 5th wrangler is relative and states nothing exactly ; it makes no mention of his intelligence, capacity for work, perseverance, even luck, and a thousand things that contributed to make up the number of marks which decided his relative posi-

tion ; it is, in fact, a sort of approximate comparison and judgment regarding one candidate
and other candidates in special circumstances.
(Obviously no criticism is intended of this method,
nor of the use which is made in language of ordinal numbers.) Therefore, an ordinal number
is not an entity ; it is a symbol, a sort of mental
crutch which men must needs call to their aid
where more exactness, or rather completeness, is
out of the question. At the risk of being weari-
some we will give another example. " The first
and last man in a procession." These terms are
a mental representation of a man's relative position in a line of men. But, tested by reality,
what are they ? Men are seen walking in line,
one behind the other ; the first man has no one
in front of him, the last man has no one behind him.
If it is said of the first man that he has more air
to breathe, that is a fact or reality due to his relative position, but independent of the number
" one " or " first," which has been tacked on to
him as a help to thought, for thought becomes
easier by means of abstraction, because all but
the facts abstracted are left out of the mental

process. So numbers, cardinal and ordinal, are an abstract language (evolved by men like any other language) except when numbers represent relations and proportions in nature or in mathematics, in which case they are entities because of the different results which ensue from a different number of units.[1]

[1]If nature has a mathematical basis, and if the hypothesis of one or more units is granted, are the great physical facts or laws discovered by Newton and modified by Einstein and others, are these facts nature's way of stating a different aspect, or a metamorphosis, of the same thing ? In other words, does nature lend herself to deductive reasoning ? This would seem to be a possible interpretation of some phenomena.

# THE QUANTUM THEORY

A suggestion, with apologies to physicists and
others.

*" Fools rush in where angels fear to tread "*

IT is daring, not to say impertinent, on the part
of one who is not a scientist to touch this subject of quanta, still in its infancy, and on which
men of science have not said their last word.   As
an excuse, it is pleaded that philosophers are so
far privileged persons that their methods are
different from scientific methods and that they
are almost bound to seize upon any new discovery
or hypothesis, in the hope that such discovery
may fit in with their theories of the universe.

It would appear that events, or energy, are
separated in sequence by what might be called
intervals (of time and space ?) and proceed by
jerks.   Given that this discontinuity is inherent

in the energy of matter, it is suggested that the
ether which, by hypothesis, pervades extension
of matter as well as " space," may also fill in the
discontinuity of energy, pointing to the conclusion that, even as there is no infinity in smallness of " matter " and that there must be an in-
divisible smallest particle, even so there should be
no infinity in the divisibility of energy ; hence
energy might logically proceed by jerks ; if, on
the contrary, energy is continuous, the corollary
would be infinite divisibility, and this idea, in
connection with matter or energy, seems to belong
to the category of abstractions of the mind.   The
idea that the gaps in continuity are filled up by
ether is a mere hypothesis, which has, no doubt,
been suggested before.  Supposing that ether
does fill in such jerks or gaps as divide energy
and matter, the question arises as to the nature of
ether, and whether ether itself is discontinuous.
If continuous, it would seem to be of a different
" texture " from matter and infinitely divisible (?).
If discontinuous, do its particles touch ?  This
problem may interest metaphysicians pending a
decision from men of science.   For the former the

speculation about infinity in smallness is of supreme interest, but it is probable that it will never be conclusively answered. Such infinity is, of course, different from infinity in space and time, about which the writer has recorded his views. Judging by analogy, he is disposed to believe in a final smallest particle, even in ether.[1]

[1]Since writing the above, the author has seen a letter by an eminent man of science suggesting a close connection between matter, energy and ether.

# SOME ASPECTS OF MUSIC

ORDERED sounds and time intervals are the substance of music and its form. By ordered sounds is meant, speaking generally, the diatonic scale[1] and its derivatives ; by time intervals, the rhythm prompted by the melody, though in truth melody and rhythm are created together. For they are inseparable, an entity ; both are the mind and matter of which music consists, and they are welded into one by the alchemy of the composer's brain. So rhythm and tune are the substance and form of music, the products of musical emotions and the cause of musical emotions. " Pure music " is here alone in question, and the point to which it is desired to call attention is that musical emotion may be independent of all but musical ideas—in contradistinction to extraneous ideas—both in composer

[1]See " Sense of Beauty " for the origin of the musical scale. page 84.

and listener, although the state of mind, even the state of health of the composer, may influence his work.    Indeed any passion or emotion can affect it, but there is a difference between a state of mind and what is usually called an idea ; and our theory is that a musical idea is nothing other than music and is the composer's mode of self-expression, not indeed so definite as words, but equally comprehensive.    To this rule there are exceptions, and of these the dance, the lullaby and the march are instances.    Dance music is directly suggestive of dancing and of the idea of dancing, because of its sprightly rhythm and the natural pleasure people take in moving in time to music of that description.    The lullaby has a soothing repetition of melody and rhythm and suggests sleep, if for no other reason than that it is apt to induce sleep in the listener.    The march, with its incisive beat approaching to exactness or regularity, suggests ideas of energetic action or of war, because it stimulates in the hearer energetic movements of the body, as well as a feeling of mental energy.

Even " programme " music must be included in the rule that music is independent of any but musical ideas. True, the thoughts which the composer has associated with his " programme " may have vaguely influenced his composition, but the listener will be none the wiser as to the meaning associated with the work, unless he has been informed beforehand about the " programme." This experiment has often been tried and always with negative results. The same rule applies to operatic music and to oratorios (if unaccompanied by words), also to symphonies, except when the music is imitative, as in Beethoven's Pastoral Symphony and so on. With regard to much religious music, it certainly may give rise in some people to a semi-religious state of mind, but in this connection it must be remembered that such music is mostly slow, calm, sonorous and, as music, noble ; also it would be heard in church where the surroundings suggest religious ideas. Possibly, too, the emotion which religious music arouses in certain people is the nearest approach to religious feelings that they have known ; and they would therefore be unable to distinguish between musico-religious emotion and a real religious feeling, in which latter state of mind the music would be only disturbing ; for music is one thing and religion is another. In the last quoted instance, therefore, the ideas have been separately suggested to the listener and are not the direct outcome of the music. For music is a language, not a translation. This language, this " material " medium, has sufficed for a genius like Bach to stamp his personality on his own and succeeding generations as forcibly as if he had been a poet or a philosopher. His music—which is a replica of himself—expresses a great man. The notes and rhythm, which together are the music, have been welded in the composer's brain ; otherwise there would have been sounds and un-meaning time intervals, not music ; for music is man-made.

A technical point may be mentioned, although it is a digression, as it may interest some music lovers. It is well known that the diatonic scale has a mathematical basis, but the number of har-monics or overtones which accompany the notes seem to preclude the scale, as used by instruments, from ranking as mathematically exact. Keyed instruments have to be tuned differently from the

diatonic scale for practical reasons.[1]   The inex-
actness of rhythm is more easy to distinguish and
to explain.   It has, so to say, an exact basis,
which may be called its skeleton.   This skeleton
must dominate the rhythm and yet be hidden,
which is the fate of all skeletons.   Whether
composing or playing, the musician feels the
beat—the skeleton—as well as the rhythm
which the melody imposes, and his general
" tempo " remains the same throughout.   Music
is typical in this respect of a remarkable char-
acteristic of man, that of making abstractions
from realities, while being at the same time in-
tensely conscious of those realities by means of
his intuitions, artistic and other.   The musician
abstracts the regular beat—the skeleton—and
subordinates it at will to the rhythm of the tune—
a feat of musicianship comparable to that of playing two or more games of chess at a sitting.   These
two so different time-ideas he holds concurrently,
whether consciously or not.   To realize how im-

[1]On these instruments the octave is divided into twelve
equal semitones ; this way of tuning is a necessary compromise in
order to make our complicated harmony possible with the
limited number of notes on keyed instruments.

possible it is to play a melody musically in exact
instead of in rhythmic time, it suffices to use a
" metronome." But possibly the feeling for
exact time is more than abstraction from melodic
or other rhythm, and is in some way connected with
psychology, or even with physiology. For it is a
talent to be able to abstract exact time from rhythm
in order to maintain the tempo, a talent which
some musicians lack. Yet it is probable that
musical people detect better than unmusical ones
any slight irregularity in, for instance, the beat
of a pendulum. This fact seems to indicate that
in the musician it is a case of abstraction which
results from his habit of distinguishing between
rhythm and exact time, the feeling for both of
which is required in music. There is also a sense
of the lapse of time unconnected with music ;
some persons will wake up each morning at the
same hour ; others, if they awake in the night,
will know what time it is. Many labourers
engaged at their work guess the time with curious
accuracy, especially the hour when work should
cease ; this is to be taken seriously, for we speak
of a real faculty that not all workmen possess.

These cases are mentioned, not in connection with abstractions from rhythm, although they might come under this head—we know not—but as being a true sense of the lapse of time, due no doubt to complex causes.

To resume and sum up : there is in music a close connection between mind and matter, not to say an identity for the reasons that, in music, form and substance are one, and that the " material " medium of music is as significant of thought and emotion as the definite ideas conveyed by the symbol of words. So music stands apart ; a compound of mind and matter, like the human complex of which it is an epitome, and it rests upon the world like a breath from the gods.

But it makes alike for good and evil, in that it rises to sublime heights, or sinks to the level of vulgar platitudes. Yet mainly it works for good. It is the antithesis of anarchism, because, even in its most feeble attempts, it is obedient to law ; keeping within the bounds of rhythmic time, and of ordered intervals.

# ETHICS

IT would seem natural that men of such divergent opinions as determinists and transcendentalists should cherish different ideals, which in turn might be expected to affect their actions. Yet it is a fact that when these opposing philosophies are translated into conduct, the difference in the result is very small. The transcendentalist might well claim ethics as his preserve because a moral law is enforced by religions, and is usually associated with a belief in spirit apart from matter, a belief in good and evil, and particularly in free will, of which he might assert that it is the " *sine qua non* " of morality. And as it is true that ethics and free will do each connote the other, the logic of the transcendentalist in this respect appears to be unassailable.

Quite other is the standpoint of the determinist ; and thus the problem is why he draws similar conclusions—if conduct is a test—although he starts from such different premises. In order to throw some light upon it, by comparing the two philosophies, and also as an illustration of their possible effect upon character, we have selected ordinary types and characters, and have suggested the arguments that might be advanced on both sides in support of the respective theories. The human illustrations are useful because ethics cannot be treated apart from psychology : Imagine, then, an individual, a transcendentalist who believes in a moral law, and desires to conform to it. Such a man may nevertheless be much hated, and with good cause. If he should lack some particular virtue, he will need constant self-control in order to conform to his own standard of right conduct. Let the virtue in question be generosity and suppose our moralist to be, by nature or education, miserly. He will make painful efforts to overcome his avarice, with the result that he will estrange the recipients of his bounty. For the latter will rarely be deceived and will resent a gift grudgingly bestowed ; they will feel it as an affront and will dislike the donor. The effect on our moralist will be one of mingled feelings ; he will rejoice to have acted in accordance with his lights, yet he will be conscious that his temper has suffered in the process, and further that he has earned no gratitude in return for his generosity. It is true that such bounties are mostly conferred on institutions—as they can then take the impersonal form of a cheque through a secretary—rather than on a friend or relative who would expect some mark of affection to accompany the gift, and as our merely moral man has difficulty in attuning himself to the required mood, he will avoid occasions which would make demands upon his graciousness. From which it may be concluded that men such as he fail in the qualities of sympathy and love. Indeed this was implied in the statement that our moral man was avaricious, for love and avarice are not boon companions.

Now most codes of morals prescribe love and sympathy, but love is elusive and so is sympathy, and as our moralist is unable either to command or feign these virtues, he rouses feelings of dislike instead of affection. Love therefore is indispensable not only to a code of morals, but likewise to all would-be benefactors, and unfor-

tunately it is just love which free will, inseparable
from ethics, is unable to command. Notwithstanding this weak point in his armour, the code
of morals of the transcendentalist is no doubt a
source of strength to him, and it is also possible—
an important point—that his self-control increases
by use.

Meanwhile the determinist must steer a course
without the help of rules ; as he denies free will,
he has no reason to obey a moral code ; hence, if
he is to explain to himself and to the world why he
values those virtues and ideals which, according
to his view, he is incapable of making any effort
to attain, he must fall back upon heredity, education, surroundings, and especially love, which he
may claim as part of his inheritance. He may
even assert that love alone is a sufficient motive
for all virtue, and stands independent of dogma.
If we suppose him in conversation with his friend
a transcendentalist, the latter might reply to this
assertion : " But all men are not moved by love,
and therefore they need rules of conduct. They
must be told to worship God and learn how to
love, to frequent those who suffer and learn pity,

to live amongst beautiful things and be moved to admiration." To which the determinist : " If I worship God because you bid me, it is either that your command is for me a new motive, or that, perchance, I already know the power of prayer, for I am the puppet of forces within and without. As to pity, my nature is such that I avoid the sight of pain, yet it may be that the fear of your censure being now a fresh motive, will induce me to frequent those who suffer. In that case the ' merit ' if any, will be yours. But should the sight of suffering indeed call forth my pity, no doubt the pain to myself will deter me from repeating the experiment. As to beautiful objects, I feel no desire to be near them, but again, as I am anxious to meet with your approval, I shall approach them, and possibly I shall enjoy the sight or sound of what you call ' beautiful.' Then the memory of my pleasure will move me to return. But still I shall be a puppet, of which you, amongst other forces, will be pulling the strings."

Notwithstanding such arguments, a determinist of good instincts and upbringing is bound to heave many a sigh at the thought that he is

powerless to guide himself and shape his conduct.
He must often wish that he did believe in responsibility, and feel that the mere fact of believing
would in itself be a lever on the side of right action;
he may even decide to act in future as if he did so
believe, while at the same time feeling confident
that what he suffers through his conviction of im-
potence is the real motive that now urges him to a
make-believe which he has decided upon because
he thinks it is a power for good.  This self-
analysis could be expressed thus : " I know I am
a puppet, yet I intend to act as if I were free by
pretending that I am free, but in taking this decision I am not free, for everything I do is only a
yielding to the strongest motive."  Again it is
true that our friend's good intentions would soon
by force of habit bring him very near to the transcendentalist in feeling and conduct.  As to his
logic, it must be confessed to be sound.  The
foregoing may help to explain how men of similar
instincts, but opposing theories, are prone to agree
in conduct and even in ideals—if a determinist
can be said to have ideals.

But there is another aspect of the problem :

what are the moral effects of a belief in free will
and a moral code apart from the inquiry whether
such beliefs are a true conception of the facts of
life ? Thus to shift the ground from a search
after truth to one of expediency demands an ac-
knowledgment and an apology, but the inquiry
can scarcely be left out when the subject is ethics.
The influence for good of a belief in free will and
a moral law on the great majority of people will
probably not be disputed. Unfortunately, rules
of conduct are not always good. Evil doctrines
are much preached, to the danger of peoples and
institutions, and as a belief in free will has the
effect of strengthening the will, the result in these
circumstances is evil. Yet there is reason to
believe that more good than evil doctrines are
spread, so that on this count the argument would
be favourable to the transcendentalist and his
teaching of personal responsibility.[1]

[1] The modern tendency to treat criminals, and even children, as if society, not they, were responsible, is a determinist's
attitude, because he would consider crime and misconduct were
due to causes outside of their own control, whereas the transcendentalist would probably divide the responsibility between
society and the criminal, between parents and children, the
government and the governed.

If it is now asked what the verdict is, the answer may well be, " If you love what is good you will be saved either way." To which must be added that a thought is a force, and that a man who believes in love as a motive throws his weight in the balance for good, even if he should have no belief in responsibility. Also his task is harder than the transcendentalist's, for " he walks straight without a crutch." Of self-sacrifice, it might be alleged that only such as obey a moral law can be prepared to sacrifice themselves. This is not so, or if the denial must be qualified, let it be put in this way : A man who obeys a moral law is better equipped to make sacrifices for those whom he does *not* love, but both he and his opponent in philosophy share with all living creatures the most widespread mode of self-sacrifice, that of the parent for the offspring, and that of the male for the defence of the home. Such sacrifice is independent of a moral code ; in other words, where there is love, there is no sacrifice, an argument which must not be pursued further under penalty of having to define sacrifice. A touching instance is that of Abraham, who loved Isaac much, but loved God more.

It must be admitted that neither school of thought can prove its assertions. One or other will be believed, according to the disposition and upbringing of the thinker. As to the question whether it is well to believe in responsibility, the reply is yes, because a belief in freedom makes of men more potent agents for either good or evil, and we opine that there is more good than evil in the world.

# LANGUAGE AND LAUGHTER

LANGUAGE is a factor in the foundation of our beliefs, for a philosophy is implicit in many words commonly used. The words " duty" and " responsibility " convey the idea of free will, of a moral law and of man's power to obey or disobey it. It is probable, for instance, that the word " duty " and the idea connected with it act and react on each other, and that it influences men from childhood. Language has a direct influence on thought, and thought on language, and language makes and moulds the thoughts of children and men.

If fatalists use such words as duty and responsibility in the ordinary sense—free will and fate being incompatible [1]—they must believe that Providence constantly interferes in the affairs of men, otherwise their theory would be inconsistent. For a man cannot be fated to be drowned and be

[1] Ethics, page 68.

at the same time free to take such steps as will ensure his safety, unless it is thought that Providence, while allowing him apparent freedom, thwarts him in the end by some miracle.

Many words have been handed down to us with the ideas which formed the words, and which, in turn, they form. " Cause " and " effect " are a philosophy. A different philosophy replaces them by " sequence of events." With regard to the word " duty," it is not alleged that the feeling might not exist without the knowledge of the word. Indeed a dog may be said to have a sense of duty or of justice ; he looks " guilty " when he has stolen a bone. Yet the fact remains that language is indispensable to men for complex or continuous thought. In the same way, numbers, which are symbols, like language, are indispensable for reckoning,[1] even as notation is necessary for complex music. Thus regarded, language is both our master and our servant.

It will be objected that feeling does on occasion precede thought and that in such case, thought can

[1]With certain remarkable exceptions, namely the intuitive faculty for numbers.

owe nothing to language.  This is true, for without mentioning the obvious instance of our senses, feeling may precede thought in intellectual phenomena, as when a logical man feels a fallacy before he has had time to formulate it : he feels it as an intellectual annoyance or challenge.  It is not quite clear whether the feeling results from the effort to detect the fallacy, or whether a fallacy by its nature is painful to a logical mind.  Possibly feeling and thought may be the same phenomenon at different stages.  However that may be, the rule holds good with few exceptions, that language is indispensable for thought.  The two usual acceptations of the word " reflection " will also serve as an example of philosophy implicit in words.  For they are not merely a figure of speech. If it were doubtful whether these two thought-processes could be distinguished, namely, the imaginative one which sees a resemblance and uses a word in a figurative sense, and the philosophical one which feels a deeper meaning, welds thought and word into one and so constructs a philosophy of language, the answer would be found in the word itself.  For " reflection " means, first,

a physical effect, as when an object is duplicated
in a pool, and secondly it means a mental process,
as when the mind recalls objects seen or heard,
or, again abstract ideas and reasons about them.
Both the physical and mental processes are replicas of the original object, and in this consists the
identity, or similarity. This sense of their similarity is a philosophy. The word " impression "
is a parallel case, even if it be called a figure of
speech. There is the impression in wax and the
impression on the brain of any physical or mental
phenomenon. Both are replicas of the object.
Such instances could be multiplied without end.
The word " relaxation " must be treated at greater
length as " Laughter."

Laughter appears to be a relaxation of the physical and mental muscles. The word " relaxation " means amusement and pleasure, as well as
absence or cessation of effort. It is an instance
of the philosophy and unconscious psychology of
language. Spectators at a game of tennis will
laugh should one of the players slip and fall. The
reason is that they have been following and men-
tally playing the game, and they are alert ; when

the player falls, the strained attention of the on-
looker is suddenly checked and diverted—*i.e.*,
relaxed, and laughter follows. In every farcical
situation it will be found that the attention or
alertness of the audience is diverted from the expected action of the play or story, and is thus relaxed : when the comical character suddenly
appears on the stage dressed in eccentric or
startling garments, attention is diverted from
the story to the staring pattern of the actor's
clothes.

It is said of an experienced teacher at a gym-
nasium in Paris that he invariably warned his pupils
not to laugh when muscular effort was required ;
he knew that laughter meant " relaxation " of the
muscles. Another teacher, whose juvenile class
was now and then seized with uncontrollable
fits of laughter, would wait patiently and bid his
pupils have their laugh out. This permission to
laugh was helpful, because it diverted their minds
from any trivial matter that had started them off,
thus changing the direction of their thoughts
from the subject of laughter to his sanction to
laugh, as well as suggesting a return to work after

the laugh was over. If he had reproved them, the little strength that was left for self-control through the relaxation of laughter, would have been diminished by fear of his displeasure. Whether or not this is the true explanation, his method always succeeded.

Seriousness precedes and accompanies every effort or emotion. " Stiffen the sinews. . . ." Art is serious, as are war, anger, love, ambition, admiration, all striving, all honest work, all games of skill, and so on. At a match of billiards, chess, tennis, polo and other games both mental and physical, a smile will never be seen on the faces of the players. The French were wont to say that in England we took our pleasures sadly, meaning our games ; they should have said seriously. This is true, and for the reason that our games are strenuous. So an explanation of the phenomenon of laughter seems to be a sudden arrest of effort—physical or mental—or the diverting of attention, resulting in relaxation. Bergson, in his treatise on laughter, gives an elaborate but scarcely convincing explanation. Our suggestion can be put to the test by anyone who cares to do so, but it is not always easy to discover the cause of the relaxation.[1]

[1]It is probable that the author of a farce and the actor are serious when writing and acting, because they are doing strenuous work.  At times an actor will be seen to smile at a fellow actor's jokes, but rarely, if ever, at his own, unless the play demands it.

# THE SENSE OF BEAUTY

IT was suggested in *The Modern Churchman* of September, 1924, that the sense of beauty had never been accounted for, and this argument was used in support of a transcendental philosophy.

Although the writer claims to be a transcendentalist, he does not admit that the sense of beauty cannot be accounted for. An attempt will be made in the following pages to describe by what means he believes it to have been evolved, or, in other words, to show the close connection that exists between Usefulness on the one hand, and Symmetry, Balance, Colour and Expressiveness on the other, to which must be added Melody and Rhythm. All these factors, including usefulness, have combined to form what is called a Sense of Beauty. Indeed so close is the connection that it is difficult to speak separately of Usefulness. It may be stated at once that Love must be included as a useful quality, although it is not usually spoken of as such. But in fact it is the most indispensable of all factors in the rearing of a family and for the survival of a race. Its connection with the Sense of Beauty will be pointed out. The theory is that Symmetry, Balance, Colour, Expressiveness, as well as Melody and Rhythm (which together are Music) have been evolved for their usefulness, while the Sense of the Beauty of those factors has arisen from the pleasurable emotions of love, friendship, familiarity and safety associated with them, for it will not be denied that a sense of beauty is in its nature pleasurable. No definition of it would be complete, or psychologically true, if the pleasure which accompanies it were ignored.

It is well known that the life of a plant or tree is a struggle for air, light and moisture in all directions. Above ground the branches extend for air and light. Below ground the roots spread for moisture and firmness. A perfect balance is the result where growth is not checked by vegetation or other obstructions. Symmetry and balance are equally necessary for men and the lower animals. They are present in nearly all living

things, and naturally.   Man and beast need them
for every sort of exercise and movement, especially for attack and for defence ;  birds need them
for their flight through the air, fishes for swimming
in rivers and seas, and so on.   Their usefulness,
therefore, will not be disputed, and will account
for the evolution of symmetry and balance.

The first step in man towards a sense of the
beauty of symmetry would have been the love of
the young child for this attribute of all the organisms surrounding it, more especially the symmetry
of its mother's face and limbs, and even of its
own little body.   An early habit of mind would
have been formed associating symmetry with love,
familiarity and the security of home.   Even the
child's vocabulary witnesses to the close connection in its mind between what it likes and its sense
of beauty.   It says " beautiful " of any pleasurable sensation, whether of objects seen, heard or
tasted, nor is the word used in a merely figurative
sense.   The ideas are so firmly associated in its
mind that it uses for them the same expressions.[1]
Not only the child, but also primitive and un-

[1]See " Language," page 77.

trained adults, take pleasure in straight and sym-
metrical lines. These lines are further appreciated for their usefulness, as when a man who
is clearing up a shed, will put boxes or bricks
square with the wall, and will at times stop to
admire his work. In this he shows a primitive
sense of beauty associated, in this case, with a
feeling of usefulness and roominess. It is scarcely
necessary to point out that such a primitive sense
of beauty as that of mere regularity becomes a
more complex and refined appreciation as men
themselves become more complex and refined.

With regard to the usefulness of colour to men
and animals, by contrast or similarity, and the
usefulness of sounds, as warnings or friendly calls,
these points come under expressiveness ; but the
sense of the beauty of colour will be considered
first, and the sense of the beauty of sound and
rhythm will be dealt with later. The infant has
seen and loved colour in its mother's face, as in
all its home surroundings, and it will still love
colour for that reason. It loves what it is familiar
with, and it admires what it loves. Adults are
equally susceptible to such association of ideas.

The love of colour is very widespread. It is attributed even to insects, and has probably been evolved in part for its usefulness, which is to say that both the colour and the love of colour may have their uses ; an instance of the latter might be the love of bees for the colour of flowers.

Darwin has shown how important is colour for the safety of insects. These have learnt to associate some colours with safety for themselves, while other colours have enabled them to distinguish their prey, and a primitive sense of beauty may have been evolved, even in insects, through association with usefulness.

Expressiveness or significance, which is admittedly a beauty in art, is useful to man and beast, as it helps to distinguish friends from foes as by threatening or conciliatory gestures. There is also expressiveness through contrast of colour. This is useful for distinguishing an enemy perceived more clearly against a darker or lighter background, a fact which was made use of in the Great War and gave many opportunities for " camouflage." There is the usefulness of similarity of colour for escaping the notice of foes, or for approaching almost unseen a desired prey. The polar bear is nearly indistinguishable against the snow of his native haunts.

The late celebrated sculptor, A. von Hildebrand, in a small treatise on art, pointed out the distinctness of form which results from contrasting colours, as when the walls of a house are different in colour from its roof.   Indeed he mentions Expressiveness far more than beauty as an aesthetic quality.   But the two cannot be divorced, nor their connection with usefulness.   They are like different facets of a diamond.

The late Sir W. Armstrong states in his *Life of Gainsborough* that an object is beautiful because it looks useful ;  a church spire suggests thoughts of heaven by directing men's vision upwards.   A yacht flying before the wind is beautiful because its sails are seen to be shaped to hold the wind and their usefulness is visible.   On the other hand, and in contrast to these instances, which are thereby emphasized, machinery is ugly, for although it is known to be useful, its form does not express usefulness.

The most complete form of expressiveness is,

of course, spoken language, the usefulness of which needs no comment.   Other forms of expressiveness are visible signs, such as smiles and frowns, aural ones like laughter and growls, and all the notes of birds and beasts signifying joy, fear, hunger, anger, and so on.   There are indeed innumerable sounds which form an inarticulate, but useful, language.   The frown and the growl and all signs of anger would not be thought beautiful (except in art, for their significance) because they would rouse painful emotions and, as already stated, the sense of beauty must be linked to a feeling of pleasure, but their usefulness as a warning would be felt and appreciated.

The voice was the earliest musical instrument. It is known that the diatonic scale is developed from the harmonics or overtones of a few single notes.[1]   This scale, or some notes of it, must have been discovered early in the civilization of man through the acuteness of his senses.   The scale, once discovered, would have interested and amused him and would have been a first and important step towards the discovery of a simple melody, or

[1]See " Some Aspects of Music " page 61.

at any rate of some combination of successive notes. It would have whiled away the tedium of idle hours and in this way a primitive musical art would have become associated with family and home. The mother would have shared in the pastime, and her gentle tones would have repeated with regularity or rhythm a simple melody. For she would soon have discovered how soothing is rhythm to a fretful babe, and thus, in many a home, the lullaby would have been born. We all know how pleasant is a soft and evenly recurring note ; how soothing, because expected ; and how disturbing is an intermittent sound, because unrhythmic and unexpected. Indeed this principle is of wide application. A horse works cheerfully at an expected task and gets through his usual routine without fatigue, whereas he becomes restive at any strange and unexpected command. A child listens eagerly to familiar tales and prefers to hear the same story repeated if possible in the same words. No doubt this was true of those simple tunes and early, restful lullabies that echoed in the dwellings or caves of our forebears. They may well have been one of the first steps in the evolution of the sense of beauty in music.[1]

No mention has been made so far of poetry and literature and of beauty in connection with them, and the analysis of these subjects must be left to persons who have made of them a life study, but the writer has little doubt that the same principle applies to them as to all the arts.

Here, a distinction must be made between beauty and the sense of beauty. The writer contends that beauty does not exist apart from the sense of beauty. A work of art is a thing of beauty because it is the outcome of that sense of beauty which has been evolved in man through the associations already mentioned and in the course of ages. A beautiful work created by man is a replica of his emotions, a part of himself, a product of his brain. Thus it is scarcely a separ-

[1]The theories suggested above point to an analogy between rhythm, straight lines and numbers—things heard, seen and counted. In all three regularity is required for measurement; call it a unit. This requirement is psychological rather than actual. Numbers are identical with linear measurement if consecutive bricks are placed in line, when they are thought of either as numbers or length, and the rhythm of music, although melodic, is felt to have an underlying regular basis, and is counted as beats and bars. (See " Music," page 61).

ate entity—as beauty. True, it survives him and is thus comparable to a crystallized sense of beauty, but the appreciation of other men is necessary to recreate it as beauty, as part of the stream of living beauty. What is called the beauty of nature has been evolved, as already shown, for its usefulness, as in the case of symmetry, colour and expressiveness. Man reads beauty into nature and makes of her his medium for revealing or expressing himself, as when from sounds he creates music. In conclusion, it may be said that the sense of beauty is born of love, even as love is born of the sense of beauty.[1]

[1]See Darwin's *Origin of Species* on love and music.

## SOME OF OUR FACULTIES

THERE seems to be no reason why men in favourable world circumstances should not eventually become supermen, why their faculties should not develop, some that are now latent growing into activity in a normal way.

The late Lawrence Oliphant, who seemed to possess faculties which are absent or dormant in the great majority of men, told the writer that he was more conscious of these (occult) faculties or consciousness when he lived in the East than in Europe. Doubtless the circumstances were favourable. History and science testify to progress in man. Our forebears were savages and had developed from even lower types. Some doctors state that the children of to-day are more " brainy " than they were in the last generation. The average span of life has increased. It is said that ancient armour is too small for men of our day. Medicine and surgery have made enormous strides ; more attention is being paid to the psychology of the child, to the choice of careers, to industrial fatigue and kindred subjects. All such advances in knowledge tend towards physical and mental progress and make it possible to hope that our faculties will grow, and that perhaps new ones will emerge. But such a renaissance must depend upon the future of the world. If there should be no progress in public opinion on such problems as education, including ethics ; on sociology, war, industrial disputes ; no balanced judgment on patriotic nationalism and class internationalism, as well as on many other questions vital to the well-being of man, our planet will be the scene of renewed wars and disputes, and there will be a set-back to civilization. The improvement of the individual will be postponed indefinitely, and the superman will remain a dream.

Meanwhile, our faculties at their present stage of development are worth attention. All artistic feeling, religious emotion and such almost inborn feelings as a sense of justice and a horror of cruelty may be ranked as intuitive faculties, for they are, or seem to be, native to some persons. It is true that less well endowed natures are predisposed to cruelty, but these are probably a minority, and it seems possible that love of cruelty may be the result of bad education, and is simply a craving for excitement to which might have been given a different outlet. Of other faculties or talents which may be developed now or in the future, one is telepathy. It would be well if persons who believe that they have had telepathic experiences would record them. All such records are valuable, less so, perhaps, when they speak of experiments made with a view to getting definite results or proofs (as the state of mind induced by this " scientific " attitude is apt to defeat its end), than when they relate to unsought and unexpected experiences. For telepathy is more likely to occur to persons in a relaxed state of mind ; and their experiences would probably be more interesting than any experimental telepathy could be, for the reason given. Also testimony in favour of telepathy from trustworthy persons must be useful as an illustration that " nature makes no leaps," in other words, that mind and matter may be one or closely related or inseparable, a conclusion which would help to solve many problems in philosophy. Telepathy may be a perfectly normal psychic phenomenon, at present little developed, but capable of further development. One might conceive it as a form of physiological electricity, as a force, a system of wireless from brain to brain ; not the wireless we know, but some medium yet unprobed. Such a hypothesis, which would account for the seeming mystery, would naturally be rejected by all schools of philosophy who hold that thought cannot be transmitted by anything analogous to material forces other than language, which is a symbol ; but the last word has not been said on the transformation of physical into mental energy, nor on their possible identity. Other faculties or senses there may be that partake of mental and physical attributes. Of one of these mention will be made. It recalls the sense of music, yet it is different and it is not easy to describe. Nor is this surprising, for it would be equally difficult to describe sweetness or colour to anyone who had never tasted sugar or who was blind. The sense in question may be first felt in childhood ; it does not appear to have any traceable objective cause ; it comes and goes without warning, in which respect it somewhat resembles a dream ; yet it is not a dream, nor is it felt during sleep ; it passes like a wave of sensation, lasts a few seconds and is gone, is always welcome, is not sensual ; does not vary, and thus becomes associated with memory, linking together a whole life, and re-calling feelings and scenes of childhood—it is pleasurable but not gross, and in that respect it is like music. It is felt when health is at its best ; comes seldom and unexpectedly. It is rarely felt when one is in company, or much absorbed or excited or ill. Probably the rush and tumble of life is antagonistic to the feeling in question as to much else in us that would be for our good. As evidence of this, it may be recalled how, upon awaking, one understands easily some point which was baffling on the previous night.

The sensation in question is a small matter and has led to nothing outside itself in the writer, but it is interesting as pointing to little known faculties, also perhaps to the importance of leisure for physical and mental development. For it is doubtful whether any rare sense or talent could emerge amid bustle and constant excitement, and may be, if it did, it would be harmful to its possessor.

Possibly, though not probably, the faculty described is subconscious memory, not defined enough to form ideas and, therefore, manifested as sensation. Yet if this were so, a feeling of depression might also be attibuted to subconscious memory. But there is a difference in the two phenomena : the pleasurable feeling comes as a wave, while depression is usually static ; also the latter can generally be explained by some known cause.

# APPENDIX

## TELEPATHY

TELEPATHY may be an undeveloped sense, or a rudimentary one. It may be of the same nature as other senses, or physiologically different. Probably animals have the faculty to some extent, and this is the more likely that it seems to be independent of words. Many persons disbelieve in telepathy, although there is reliable evidence in support of it ; evidence which it would be difficult to account for by coincidence or imagination. If telepathy is akin to other senses, it has doubtless been evolved for its usefulness, but it may also have become rudimentary if and when it ceased to be useful. Civilization in man and domestication in animals have tended to blunt some senses as danger decreased. Unfavourable circumstances have a similar effect, as when the student's work leads to shortness of sight, in contrast to the sailor's long vision.[1]    But telepathy seems to be more tenuous than other senses, and it may belong to a different order of faculties.   If it is valuable, one may reasonably hope that it will be further developed.   The cases recorded below are of small interest, except for their accuracy, for which the writer can vouch.

A lady was walking in Kensington Gardens, when the thought of a casual acquaintance crossed her mind.   The idea was quickly followed by the sound of her own name, and on turning round she saw the object of her thought.   On another occasion she was walking not far from the same spot when she heard her name pronounced by a friend whose voice she at once recognized.   She had time to think while turning round : " it cannot be X, for she lies ill in bed."   To her surprise there was no one near.   Later on she learnt that her sick friend had several times, in her semi-conscious state, called out her name.   The third case was as follows :   I was motoring to town from the country when

[1]It has been objected that the sailor's sight is not so long as it appears, but that he knows what objects to look for.

I was seized with violent pains. " Strange to be in such pain, yet not to feel ill," I reflected. A few days later I heard that a valued friend had died in South Africa as a result of an operation. The dates appeared to coincide approximately. I had been aware that my friend was ill, but I did not know that she was in danger. I had never before experienced pain without some known cause, nor have I done so since.

The late Sir Walter Armstrong told the writer that he could, by the exercise of will power, make his wife do as he wished ; and he quoted the following instance : he, his wife and a friend were together in the Armstrongs' sitting-room, and his wife was busy with needlework. Sir Walter wrote on a slip of paper what it was he willed his wife to do ; he then folded the paper and handed it to the friend, unobserved by his wife, who presently laid down her work and rang for coals (the coal-box was full). The friend now unfolded the paper, on which was scribbled that Lady Armstrong should ring for coals. Questioned as to why she had done so, she replied that she did not know, but that the idea had crossed her mind.